RETURN to the LORD

Daily Devotions for Lent and Easter

ERIK J. ROTTMANN

CONCORDIA PUBLISHING HOUSE · SAINT LOUIS

Ash Wednesday and the Days Following

The Force of a Command

Read Luke 13:1–5

Return to Me with all your heart, with fasting, with weeping, and with mourning; and rend your hearts and not your garments. Joel 2:12–13a

During the eighteenth and nineteenth centuries, when the British Royal Navy was at the height of its power, superior officers customarily spoke to their subordinates with great courtesies. An admiral might send the message, "My compliments to the captain. If he finds it convenient, would he please join me for dinner?" However, the invitation carried the force of a command; no captain in his right mind would ignore the admiral's invitation! It was *always* convenient to obey. Great regret would come upon the captain who refused!

So it also is with the Word of the Lord. Pastors and theologians sometimes speak about God's invitations to us. For example, Luther wrote in his Small Catechism, "God tenderly invites us to believe" (Introduction to the Lord's Prayer). However, the courteous and gracious invitations of our Divine Admiral should never be ignored, no matter how gentle or optional they might sound!

Speaking through Joel, God invited His people, "Return to Me." Like the invitation of a British admiral, God's invitation carries the force of a command. Do not ignore God's invitation to repent of sin, thus continually returning to the Christ to be saved! The call to repentance must be obeyed. Great regret will come upon those who refuse.

Help me, Lord, to return, according to Your command. Amen.

The Wisdom of the Cross

Read 1 Corinthians 1:18–25

Behold, My servant shall act wisely; He shall be high
and lifted up, and shall be exalted. Isaiah 52:13

When Isaiah said, "high and lifted up, and . . . exalted," he was speaking about our Lord's crucifixion. Jesus Himself spoke about His cross in that same manner, saying, "I, when I am lifted up from the earth, will draw all people to Myself" (John 12:32; Jesus said this "to show what kind of death He was going to die," v. 33). Speaking about the crucifixion, Isaiah wanted us to know that our Lord acted wisely when He voluntarily died for us: "Behold, My servant shall act wisely."

Death is a strange sort of wisdom, especially the terrible death of crucifixion. But the wisdom of this particular death is made clear by the resurrection. The world wants nothing to do with the resurrection. When the Word and Wisdom of the Cross is preached, the world calls it "foolishness"; the Scriptures call it "the power of God" (1 Corinthians 1:18).

Because Jesus acted wisely on the cross, His wisdom is now ours. Our Lord's wisdom comes to us through preaching, Baptism, and the Sacrament of the Altar. Thus, we become wise; thus, even the youngest, most infantile, and most freshly baptized Christian possesses more wisdom than all the philosophers in the world put together.

Give me Your Spirit, Lord, that I may remain "wise for salvation" (2 Timothy 3:15). Amen.

Marred beyond Human Semblance
Read John 19:1–11

Many were astonished at You—His appearance was
so marred, beyond human semblance, and His form
beyond that of the children of mankind. Isaiah 52:14

"Behold the man!" (John 19:5). That is what Pontius Pilate said to the chief priests and others who had brought Jesus to Pilate. Hoping to satisfy their thirst for blood, Pilate had previously turned Jesus over to his men, who flogged and tortured our Lord. Once the torture was complete, Pilate presented Jesus to His accusers, saying, "Behold the man!"

Why did Pilate say, "Behold the man"? It might have been necessary. None of our Lord's accusers—having stood face-to-face with Him—might have been able to recognize Him any longer. "Many were astonished at You." It must have been terribly difficult to look at Jesus in that moment, just prior to His final torment on the cross. "Marred, beyond human semblance, and His form beyond that of the children of mankind." Jesus was not even recognizable as a human being. "I am a worm, and not a man" (Psalm 22:6).

Being reduced to nothing, Jesus suffered to make us into something. As a result of His marred semblance of a man, He gave us the semblance of God, righteous and pure forever.

Dearest Jesus, by the power of Your marred human semblance, crucified and lifted up, give me the semblance of God, both Your Father and mine. Amen.

Startled

Read Matthew 27:45–54

So shall He sprinkle many nations. Kings shall shut
their mouths because of Him, for that which has not
been told them they see, and that which they have not
heard they understand. Isaiah 52:15

In a footnote, the English Standard Version of the Bible offers the word *startle* as an alternative for *sprinkle* in this verse: "He [Jesus] shall startle many nations; Kings shall shut their mouths because of Him." The "shut mouths" refers not to silence but to the appalling nature of our Lord's death that it would make even powerful men cover their mouths with their hands. Powerful men would stand in awe because the death of Jesus delivered a startling revelation: "that which has not been told them they see, and that which they have not heard they understand."

A Roman centurion ("ruler of one hundred") stood at the cross while Jesus died. Our Lord's suffering—together with the sign over His head, the jeers of His enemies, and the sorrow of His friends—"startled" the centurion's confession of Christ. The centurion was awed and appalled by his own work that day; "kings shall shut their mouths because of Him." However, the centurion could not remain silent. Our Lord opened the centurion's lips so that his mouth might speak praise: "Truly this was the Son of God!"

"O LORD, open my lips, and my mouth will declare Your praise" (Psalm 51:15). Amen.

Lent Week One

God's Holy Arm
Read Psalm 98

Who has believed what he has heard from us? And to whom has the arm of the Lᴏʀᴅ been revealed? Isaiah 53:1

Jesus is the arm of the Lord and the right hand of God. The heavenly Father gave all authority to Jesus (Matthew 28:18); "in Him the whole fullness of deity dwells bodily" (Colossians 2:9).

"To whom has the arm of the Lᴏʀᴅ been revealed?" Isaiah earlier answered his own question: "The Lᴏʀᴅ has bared His holy arm before the eyes of all the nations" (Isaiah 52:10). Thus, Isaiah prophesied not only that many international visitors in Jerusalem would see the death of Jesus (John 19:20; Acts 2:5) but also that the preached message of forgiveness would fill the entire creation. "Their voice goes out through all the earth, and their words to the end of the world" (Psalm 19:4; Romans 10:18).

Isaiah's first question is more sober than the second: "Who has believed what he has heard from us?" Only those to whom the miracle of faith has been given, for "faith comes from hearing, and hearing through the word of Christ" (Romans 10:17).

Lent is a time of returning. It should also be a time of thanks. We can return only because the arm of the Lord has grasped us and turned us back toward Himself.

As You call me to return, dear heavenly Father, make my returning possible by Your powerful arm, even Jesus Christ my Lord. Amen.

Hidden Majesty

Read Matthew 17:1–8

> For He grew up before Him like a young plant, and like a root out of dry ground; He had no form or majesty that we should look at Him, and no beauty that we should desire Him. Isaiah 53:2

When John the Baptist looked at those who had come to be baptized, he knew that the Promised Christ stood somewhere there in the midst of the crowd. John simply did not know which person was the Christ. "Among you stands one you do not know. . . . I myself did not know Him (John 1:26, 31).

Our Lord's body bore no indication of His divinity. His frame was not that of an Adonis. His eyes betrayed no divine spark. His skin did not glow. The divinity of Jesus could only be detected when Jesus revealed it and only to those whom He desired to see it.

"He had no form or majesty that we should look at Him, and no beauty that we should desire Him." What, therefore, has attracted us to Him who was crucified for us and for our salvation? Only the power of His Word. Only the miracle of His self-revelation. Only the testimony of His Holy Spirit, "who spoke by the prophets" (Nicene Creed).

We have been saved by the pure miracle of God; we also believe by the pure miracle of God.

O Holy Spirit, keep my eyes open to the Christ, my Lord and my God. Amen.

Cover Your Face, Not Your Ears

Read Isaiah 49:1–7

He was despised and rejected by men, a man of
sorrows and acquainted with grief; and as one from
whom men hide their faces He was despised, and we
esteemed Him not. Isaiah 53:3

Has an accident scene ever made you cover your child's eyes? Has the sight of illness or disease made you nauseous? Are there movie scenes you cannot bear to watch? Such experiences compare to the reactions created by the suffering of Jesus, "from whom men hid their faces." Our Lord had become repulsive.

The sight of our Lord's suffering was absolutely terrible, but Isaiah did not spell out all the gory details. The four Gospel writers followed suit, describing our Lord's indescribable suffering only in simple, clinical terms: "Pilate took Jesus and flogged Him" (John 19:1); "they led Him out to crucify Him" (Mark 15:20). Not atrocious details but only unadorned statements.

Isaiah might scratch his head at our Passion plays, movie portrayals, and other forms of art that attempt to depict the crucifixion of Jesus in all its horror. Why should we want to see things that others could not bear to see? Perhaps we, too, should avert our eyes from the graphic images and focus instead upon what we hear. "Faith comes from hearing, and hearing through the word of Christ" (Romans 10:17).

Help me to return, O Lord, on the basis of what I hear and not what I see. Amen.

He Carried It All

Read John 11:32–37

Surely He has borne our griefs and carried our sorrows;
yet we esteemed Him stricken, smitten by God, and
afflicted. Isaiah 53:4

John the Baptist called Jesus "the Lamb of God who takes away the sin of the world" (John 1:29). Isaiah wanted us to know that Jesus did not merely take our sins upon Himself but that He also shouldered the entire load of all sin's effects and consequences: "He has borne our griefs and carried our sorrows."

- **Sorrows:** If you have ever experienced bad feelings because of what you have done or failed to do, or if you have had reason to regret the sins of others, then you have sorrowed. Jesus carried that sorrow.

- **Griefs:** Isaiah's word for "griefs" could also be translated as "sicknesses." To be sure, sin itself causes us much grief, which is the heartache we feel as the result of a terrible loss. However, sin has also caused us all sorts of illness and disease that wreck the body, rob happiness from our lives, and lead to death—both for ourselves and for those whom we love.

Jesus carried the entire load, not merely the sin but also all of sin's consequences. Thus, we shall at last be set free from the entire load: sins forgiven, sicknesses healed, and grief consoled.

Thank You, Lord, that You bore my entire burden of sin, sorrow, and grief so that I may return unencumbered. Amen.

Maternal Repetition

Read Hebrews 5:1–10

"But he was pierced for our transgressions; He was crushed for our iniquities; upon Him was the chastisement that brought us peace, and with His wounds we are healed. Isaiah 53:5

When a mother holds and consoles her distraught baby, she will often repeat herself, gently dandling the child and saying, "There, there. Momma's got you. You're okay now. It's all right. You are safe and sound. Hush, baby, hush."

God spoke to us through Isaiah with the same sort of maternal repetitions. On the surface, God's prophet Isaiah seems to have stated three different things, but all three are essentially the same. "You're okay now. It's all right: Jesus was pierced for our transgressions. He was crushed for our iniquities. We now have peace with God because our Lord was chastised for us. Therefore, you are safe and sound: with His wounds—that is, the stroke of the whip upon our Lord's back—we are healed."

What does the child eventually do while his mother consoles him? The child becomes calm; he stops fretting and squalling; he rests peacefully in the arms of his beloved protector.

What should we do while the Lord our God speaks through Isaiah, consoling us with His maternal repetitions? The same thing: rest in peace.

For Your wounds, I thank You; for Your crushed body, I thank You; for Your wounds, I thank You, my precious Lord! Amen.

Desire to Sin

Read Romans 1:28–2:5

All we like sheep have gone astray; we have turned—
every one—to his own way; and the LORD has laid on
Him the iniquity of us all. Isaiah 53:6

On the surface, some people are clearly more sinful than others. Other people break more laws than I break, act more selfishly than I act, and do more harmful things than I do. I'm not that bad.

Despite the appearance of things, Isaiah's words hold each person guilty of sin—including the people who do not look very sinful. No matter how we act (or fail to act), we all possess the same, universal desire to sin. Isaiah's words, "every one," indict all people everywhere, including me and you. Isaiah's words, "to his [or her!] own way" indicate that our chief sin is idolatry. We each want to be our own god. We each want to choose our own path. Even after God gives us His miracle of faith in Christ, there remains something inside each of us that continually desires to reject Christ, His commands, and His promises.

When the Lutheran forefathers described our universal desire to sin, they used the Latin word *concupiscence* (Augsburg Confession II). Isaiah called that desire "iniquity." Our Lord Jesus called it His own personal burden and responsibility: "the LORD has laid on Him the iniquity of us all."

Create in me a clean heart, O Lord. Amen.

Silence Indicates Contentment

Read Hebrews 10:1–10

He was oppressed, and He was afflicted, yet He opened not His mouth; like a lamb that is led to the slaughter, and like a sheep that before its shearers is silent, so He opened not His mouth. Isaiah 53:7

Why does an infant or a toddler cry? Babies do not cry when they are content. They cry when they need something. While Christ Jesus our Lord was "oppressed, and . . . afflicted," He needed nothing.

Why does the dog bark? She barks because she is discontent; perhaps she wants to come into the house, perhaps she sees something that alarms or excites her, perhaps a distant noise is annoying her. When Jesus was led like a lamb to the slaughter, He felt no discontent and there was nothing to alarm Him.

Why do people complain? People complain because they are not happy with their situation; they want something to change. "Like a sheep that before its shearers is silent, so He [Jesus] opened not His mouth." Why was it that Jesus "opened not His mouth"? He had nothing to complain about. Nothing needed to change. There was no place else Jesus wished to be. Jesus was exactly where He wanted to be, doing exactly what He wanted to do, suffering exactly what He wanted to suffer for us and for our salvation. He was content with His situation.

By Your oppression and affliction, make me content, O Lord! Amen.

Lent
Week Two

As for His Generation, Who Considered?

Read Romans 10:5–17

By oppression and judgment He was taken away; and as for His generation, who considered that He was cut off out of the land of the living, stricken for the transgression of My people? Isaiah 53:8

The phrase "His generation" speaks about the people who witnessed our Lord's crucifixion. Isaiah was pondering the scene. As Jesus was nailed to the cross, He looked like every other person who had ever been crucified by the Romans—and there had been many! Previously, our Lord's birth had looked like every other birth of every other child ever born. So, too, His death was comparably unremarkable in the sea of blood that flowed from so many Roman crosses. "As for His generation, who considered that He was . . . stricken for the transgression of My people?" Many people heard the sermon that was posted on the cross: "Jesus, the King of the Jews" (Matthew 27:37). Only one person allowed that sermon to help him consider what was happening to Jesus: "Truly this was the Son of God!" (Matthew 27:54).

Like the soldier, we also need sermons. Without the preached Word, Jesus of Nazareth is just another guy on a cross. With the Word and the promises that flow from it, the crucified Jesus becomes our Jesus, "cut off out of the land of the living" for us.

Help me continually to return to the preached Word, O Lord. Amen.

The Value of a Rich Man

Read James 2:1–13

And they made His grave with the wicked and with a rich man in His death, although He had done no violence, and there was no deceit in His mouth. Isaiah 53:9

We all pray for daily bread, according to the command of the Lord (Matthew 6:11; Luke 11:3). Why does God give more daily bread to some people and less to others? Does God show partiality or practice favoritism?

God gives more to one and less to another for the sake of love. Suppose He gave exactly the same material wealth to every single person. How, then, would we demonstrate love? In His mercy and grace, God uses income inequality as a gift so that we would demonstrate toward one another the same sacrificial love that God in Christ has demonstrated toward us. We were not given our materials so that we may lord it over others! We were given our materials so that we may love and be loved, just as Christ loved the Church and gave Himself up for her (Ephesians 5:25). Joseph of Arimathea served the crucified Christ by providing Him with a decent burial (Matthew 27:57–60). The rich must likewise serve the poor. "You always have the poor with you" (Matthew 26:11) so that you always have someone to love.

Help me continually to return to the true purpose of my wealth, O Lord, which You have poured out abundantly upon me. Amen.

He Shall See His Offspring

Read 1 Peter 1:1–12

Yet it was the will of the Lord to crush Him, He has put Him to grief; when His soul makes an offering for guilt, He shall see His offspring; He shall prolong His days; the will of the Lord shall prosper in His hand. Isaiah 53:10

Christ Jesus our Lord never married and never physically fathered any children. When Isaiah prophesied, "He shall see His offspring," Isaiah was speaking about the hope and benefit of our Lord's resurrection from the dead. The words "when His soul makes an offering for guilt," refer to the death of Christ. But what did the prophet say would happen after Jesus died? "He shall see His offspring." Those words are resurrection words! After our Lord's eyes closed in death, they opened again that they might see!

Actually, the resurrection promise in this verse is two-fold:

- First, the resurrection of Jesus was promised in the words "He shall see."

- Second, our own personal resurrection was promised in the words "His offspring."

Isaiah calls us the offspring of Christ, not because Jesus fathered us in an earthly, physical manner, but because God the Father has "caused us to be born again to a living hope through the resurrection of Jesus Christ from the dead" (1 Peter 1:3).

Give me Your Spirit, Lord, that I may daily live in the certainty and joy of the resurrection—both Yours and mine. Amen.

Accounted Righteous
Read Romans 4:1–12

Out of the anguish of His soul He shall see and be
satisfied; by His knowledge shall the righteous one, My
servant, make many to be accounted righteous, and
He shall bear their iniquities. Isaiah 53:11

People who use credit cards can probably grasp with ease the phrase "accounted righteous." A credit card allows its user to make purchases using someone else's money. When someone buys on credit, that person makes purchases with money he or she does not have.

Isaiah promised that we would be "accounted righteous" in Christ. Stated another way, we now live in a righteousness that is not our own! In the same way that a credit card company would credit us with cash for our purchases, the sinless and perfect Christ, sacrificed for us, now likewise credits us with His righteousness. We stand before the heavenly Father in the perfection of His eternal Son!

Here is where the analogy breaks down: when we buy on credit, we must eventually pay the bill. Unlike the credit card company, Christ Jesus has not credited His righteousness to us because He expects repayment! Jesus paid the bill for us. He said from His cross, "It is finished" (John 19:30). Those words can also be translated, "Paid in full."

Thank You, Jesus, for the righteousness that You have credited to me, having paid the bill in full, so that I might not be unrighteous in the presence of Your Father. Amen.

He Shall Divide the Spoil

Read Luke 11:14–23

Therefore I will divide Him a portion with the many, and He shall divide the spoil with the strong, because He poured out His soul to death and was numbered with the transgressors; yet He bore the sin of many, and makes intercession for the transgressors. Isaiah 53:12

Christ Jesus our Lord is our champion, going out to face the terrible enemy on our behalf. Having defeated sin, death, and hell by His own death on the cross, Jesus returned to us in the power of His resurrection. In returning, He brought to us the "spoils of war." Stated another way, Jesus has delivered to us innumerable riches and wealth as a result of His glorious victory. The "spoils of war" that our Christ has divided with us include the forgiveness of our sins, the certainty of our eternal salvation, and the hope of our own resurrection from the dead.

Having won these things for us, Jesus now divides and distributes them to us through the preaching of the Word, the administration of Holy Baptism, and the service of the Lord's Supper. When we willfully absent ourselves from these things, we cannot help but grow weak. By our participation in these things, we are numbered among "the strong."

Help me, O Lord, continually to return to the preaching of Your Word and the administration of Your sacraments that I may always participate in the spoils of Your war. Amen.

Abandoned?

Read Mark 15:35–41

My God, My God, why have You forsaken Me? Why are You so far from saving Me, from the words of My groaning? Psalm 22:1

Jesus prayed these words while He hung on His cross (Matthew 27:46). Jesus might have prayed all of Psalm 22, since the entire psalm speaks in His voice about the plight of His crucifixion. However, only these first words were reported by the Gospel writers. The writers wanted to draw our attention to these words.

Had God the Father truly abandoned Jesus, His Son? No. It is also written in Psalm 22, "He [the Father] has not hidden His face from him [Jesus], but has heard, when He [Jesus] cried to Him [the Father]" (v. 24).

Why did Jesus pray, "Why have You forsaken Me?" Because it *felt* as though God had abandoned Him. Our Lord's divine power became so quiet within Him, and His crucifixion agony was so great upon Him, Jesus felt abandoned.

By suffering the sensation of abandonment, even though He was not abandoned, Jesus was joining Himself to our situation. He knows loneliness, sorrow, grief, regret, and every other abandoned feeling. Jesus wants us to know that abandonment is just a feeling! We shall never be abandoned! "He [the Father] has not hidden His face from" us but has saved us by the death of His Son.

Heavenly Father, help me to trust You—even when I feel alone. Amen.

Unanswered Prayer

Read 2 Corinthians 12:7–10

O my God, I cry by day, but You do not answer, and by night, but I find no rest. Psalm 22:2

Christians sometimes feel angry because God seems to ignore their prayers. Perhaps we prayed that a loved one would not die, but death came anyway. Perhaps we prayed for strength against a destructive habit, but the habit did not go away. Perhaps a lonely Christian prayed to depart and be with Christ, but God did not grant the request. God could have given me great relief in this or that situation, but He did not. Why? What sort of God is He, anyway?

Our God is the God of the resurrection. As Jesus suffered for us and for our salvation, He likewise prayed to His Father but received no relief. Psalm 22 is our Lord's voice: "I cry by day, but You do not answer." Why did God not answer? Because it was better for His Christ to suffer for a while, to wait upon His Father, to die, and finally to rise again. God answered His Son in due time!

Our Lord's resurrection allows us to think that God acts graciously toward us, too, when He does not answer our prayers as we desire.

Help me, dear Father, to trust that You always act according to Your grace in Christ. Help me to wait patiently for You—even if it means suffering the silence for a while. Amen.

Lent
Week Three

Enthroned Praise

Read 1 Thessalonians 2:1–13

Yet You are holy, enthroned on the praises of Israel.
Psalm 22:3

The Hebrew word for "enthroned" could also be translated as "sit upon," "remain with," or "dwell in." The King James Version states, "Thou that inhabitest the praises of Israel." *The Amplified Bible* preferred, "You Who dwell in the praises of Israel." Here is the point: God is present in the praise of His people.

The words "You are . . . enthroned on the praises of Israel" therefore teach us something about the power of God's Word in our midst:

1. We are *Israel*. God made us His chosen people, His true Israel and children of Abraham, through our Baptism into Christ. As Paul stated, "It is those of faith who are the sons of Abraham" (Galatians 3:7).

2. We *praise* when we speak or sing about the mercies of God in Christ. This happens when we pray the Divine Service or other liturgies, read the Bible stories to our children, and speak about Jesus to our friends. (None of this speaking is optional!)

3. What happens when we praise God the Holy One? He is *enthroned*, sitting, and present in our midst, "full of grace and truth" (John 1:14). "The Word is . . . in your mouth" (Romans 10:8). When the Word proceeds from our mouth, God goes to work, accomplishing what He desires!

O Lord, open my lips that my mouth may deliver Your praise—and presence—to my neighbor. Amen.

History

Read Exodus 12:33–42

In You our fathers trusted; they trusted, and You delivered them. Psalm 22:4

Our Lord's church was His grandfather's church. Jesus held the faith of His fathers, who were real, historical people. "In You our fathers trusted."

The word "our" indicates that Jesus was fully human, having a grandfather and a genealogy, just as we do. "Our fathers" indicates all those who held the faith of the Old Testament: Adam, Eve, Abraham, Sarah, Moses, Joshua, the prophets, and more. They all waited upon the Lord, placing every confidence upon His promises. Jesus, hanging on His cross, waited with them. None were disappointed: "they trusted, and You delivered them."

These words from Psalm 22, written in our Lord's voice, provide strong comfort to us in at least two ways:

- First, we are not alone in the loneliness of faith. "Behold, a great multitude that no one could number" (Revelation 7:9) has gone before us, each of them trusting the promises of God as seriously as we ourselves must trust His promises. Even Jesus was required to trust God His Father.

- Second, God's past teaches us His present and future. Our heavenly Father has never been unfaithful, and He never shall be. "They trusted, and You delivered them." God has promised to deliver us from our sins and into eternal life through the death of His Son. He shall.

Give me Your Spirit that I may trust Your faithfulness, O Lord! Amen.

Shameless

Read Psalm 6

To You they cried and were rescued; in You they trusted and were not put to shame. Psalm 22:5

There is more than one kind of shame:

- We feel ashamed of our sins, especially when they are discovered by others. Jesus "freed us from our sins by His blood" (Revelation 1:5), but we feel their shame nonetheless. We call people "shameless" who do not regret their sins.

- We also feel the shame of misplaced confidence, such as betrayal by a loved one. We end up "put to shame," humiliated.

Jesus bore our sin and shame on His cross. Jesus had no personal sin of which to be ashamed. He was, however, "put to shame," betrayed, exposed, and publicly mocked for our sake. This He willingly endured so that we could trust and not be put to shame. "In You they trusted and were not put to shame."

Jesus "endured the cross, despising the shame" (Hebrews 12:2). Jesus so despised shame that He killed it, leaving shame behind in the tomb when He rose from the dead. But He had no shame of His own. It was our shame—and the humiliation that was due to us—that Jesus killed. In so doing, Jesus gave us a new kind of shamelessness: the shameless innocence of sin forgiven. We shall never be put to shame.

Continue to wash away my sin, O Lord, that I may remain shameless forever. Amen.

Bait the Hook

Read Matthew 12:33–42

But I am a worm and not a man, scorned by mankind
and despised by the people. Psalm 22:6

When fishing, the hook must be baited with something appealing, something that the fish will wish to eat. Not any bait will do. Walleye do not respond to catfish bait, and carp do not pursue lures that were intended for muskellunge.

An Early Church theologian named Gregory of Nyssa compared our ancient enemy the devil to a great fish: Christ Jesus our Lord hid His all-powerful divinity under the cloak of our human nature, presenting Himself as "bait" to catch the "fish." Jesus was the right bait. What could be more appealing to Satan than the One whom Satan hates the most presented like fish-bait in a reduced, wounded, pitiful form for quick consumption?

Psalm 22 might even allow us to think of our Lord's cross as the great fishhook by which Satan was captured: "I am a worm and not a man." Jesus, "the worm"—that is, "His appearance was so marred, beyond human semblance, and His form beyond that of the children of mankind" (Isaiah 52:14)—was impaled upon the hook of the cross, which Satan swallowed.

What, then, is the resurrection? Our Lord landed the fish, turning it into a trophy.

"By Pontius Pilate crucified, He suffered on the Tree and died; To show of Satan's reign the end, He did into hell descend" (*The Lutheran Hymnal*, 253:3). Amen.

When No Is Blasphemy

Read Matthew 27:39–43

All who see Me mock Me; they make mouths at Me;
they wag their heads. Psalm 22:7

As Jesus hung on the cross, the passersby fulfilled Psalm 22 by "wagging their heads" at Him (Matthew 27:39). Even today, head-wagging indicates the idea of no. Those who passed by our Lord's cross were not merely mocking Him; they used their wagging heads to say no to His words. "Those who passed by derided [that is, they blasphemed, or spoke evil about] Him, wagging their heads and saying, 'You who would destroy the temple in three days and rebuild it, save Yourself!'" (Matthew 27:39; compare John 2:19–22).

We each hear things in God's Scriptures and from His pulpits that we do not enjoy hearing. Each of us has felt tempted to add no to what God has said. When we refuse His Word—either His commandment or promise—we mock Jesus in the same manner that He was mocked while on the cross. We blaspheme. We wag our heads at our crucified Lord. This is a bad situation, one from which we must turn and repent.

May God the Holy Spirit grant that we always say yes to the words of Jesus! His words deliver forgiveness and life!

I confess, O Lord, that I do not always want to hear the things You have said in Your Word. By Your grace, turn my no always into yes. Amen.

The Lord Delights in Him
Read Galatians 3:23–29

He trusts in the Lord; let Him deliver Him; let Him rescue Him, for He delights in Him! Psalm 22:8

It is difficult to see how the God of Israel could have taken delight in looking at the crucified man hanging wretchedly on the cross, Yet the words of our Psalm, even when heard out of the mouth of the accuser, always carries a degree of truth: "He delights in Him!"

The words at the end of the verse, "He delights in Him," form a bookend with the words at the beginning of the verse, "He trusts in the Lord." These two phrases depict the eternal connection between the Father and the Son: Jesus the Son trusts His Father; the Father delights in His Son. The Father did not fail to rescue the Son. The Son simply waited upon His Father's good pleasure.

"In Christ Jesus you are all sons of God, through faith" (Galatians 3:26). The word *sons* in this verse does not deny the reality of *daughters*. The word *sons* emphasizes each Christian's personal connection to the eternal Son, God the Son. Through Baptism, Jesus has come to you, giving His trust to you in order that you also may trust in His Father. Baptism indicates that it may be faithfully said concerning you, "The Father delights in you." You also may confidently wait upon the Lord.

O Lord, I trust in You. Rescue and deliver me, according to Your fatherly delight. Amen.

You Made Me Trust You

Read Hebrews 4:11–16

Yet You are He who took Me from the womb; You made
Me trust You at My mother's breasts. Psalm 22:9

Jesus is the eternal God, "equal to the Father with respect to His divinity, less than the Father with respect to His humanity," as we say in the Athanasian Creed (*LSB* 320:31). God the Son so thoroughly quieted His all-powerful divinity within His human nature that the Son became dependent upon the Father for all things—including His faith. Psalm 22 speaks the voice of Jesus, and Jesus said to His Father, "You made Me trust You at My mother's breasts."

Faith is a gift from God, a gift that must be received by means of the miracle of the Word. Like us, Jesus read His Father's Word: "He unrolled the scroll and found the place where it was written" (Luke 4:17). Like us, Jesus spoke and confessed His Father's Word: "Be gone, Satan! For it is written " (Matthew 4:10). Like us, Jesus prayed on the basis of His Father's Word: "Not My will, but Yours, be done" (Luke 22:42). Like us, Jesus also waited upon His Father's good pleasure: "You made Me trust You at My mother's breasts," and "Father, into Your hands I commit My Spirit!" (Luke 23:46).

Thus, when we must trust the Father's Word and wait upon His will, we are not alone.

By Your trust, dearest Jesus, I shall trust. Amen.

Lent
Week Four

On You Was I Cast
Read Luke 2:22–32

On You was I cast from My birth; and from My mother's
womb You have been My God. Psalm 22:10

Mary and Joseph brought their infant to the temple "to present
Him to the Lord" (Luke 2:22). Psalm 22 describes the event this way:
"On You was I cast from My birth."

Every other firstborn son in Israel was redeemed by his parents.
By making a sacrifice on that child's behalf, his parents could "buy
back" that child from the God who had said, "All the firstborn are
Mine" (Numbers 3:13). Mary and Joseph did not buy their infant
back from God. They presented Jesus to the Lord so that the Lord
would do with the Christ Child as He wished. "On You was I cast
from My birth."

Many people today refuse infant Baptism, instead "dedicating"
their children to the Lord. Such dedications are only pretend. They
not only deny the power of God's miracle of Baptism but they also
deny the incarnation of our Lord. (Old Testament rites, re-enacted or
approximated, implicitly deny the coming of Christ.)

How do godly parents cast their children onto the Lord today?
They do so through Baptism, whereby that child is eternally adopted
by God into the eternal family of God. Through Baptism, we cast our
children upon the Lord, and they land right next to Jesus.

Continually return me, and my children, to the benefit of Baptism, O Lord!
Amen.

Trouble Is Near

Read Hebrews 2:14–18

Be not far from Me, for trouble is near, and there is none to help. Psalm 22:11

Why do we lock the doors of our house? Why do we pile food in our pantry, stack junk in the garage, and keep clothes we will never wear again? What is the real purpose of insurance policies, seat belts, jumper cables, and cell phones (especially when given to six-year-olds)? Intrinsically, these things are neither bad nor good; the bad or the good consists only in the use we make of them and the trust we place in them. But why do we concern ourselves with them?

We seek after these things because "trouble is near." Trouble is always near, just around the next corner, and we want protection from it. Sometimes we can anticipate the trouble; other times we cannot. But we want to be ready for it. We want many things to be nearby and handy, in order to help us when trouble is near.

Trouble drew near to our Christ—trouble due to us rather than to Him—and there was none to help. "Many hands were raised to wound Him, None would intervene to save" (*LSB* 451:2). It had to be that way: Jesus remained alone while trouble was near in order that we never shall be alone. Because He faced our trouble all alone, we now can confidently say, "the LORD is with me" (Jeremiah 20:11).

Stay with me, Lord! Amen.

Bulls of Bashan

Read Numbers 21:31–35

Many bulls encompass Me; strong bulls of Bashan surround Me. Psalm 22:12

The imagery behind the word *Bashan* is twofold:

First, Bashan was a place well known for its grazing land. The bulls of Bashan were extremely well fed, immensely strong, and notoriously large. As a point of comparison, think of the Grand Champion Bull at your county or state fair. The "many bulls" that encompassed and surrounded Jesus were a formidable enemy, especially to one in a weakened and exposed condition.

Second, Bashan was the territory of King Og, one of ancient Israel's first and most disconcerting enemies. "Og the king of Bashan came out against them, he and all his people, to battle at Edrei" (Numbers 21:33). Although the opponent was formidable, God promised victory to Moses and the people, saying, "Do not fear him, for I have given him into your hand" (Numbers 21:34). As a result of God's promise, Moses and the people "defeated him [Og] and his sons and all his people, until he had no survivor left. And they possessed his land" (Numbers 21:35).

Although the enemy was great, encompassing and surrounding Jesus, God the Father in heaven had promised His Son the victory. Jesus is our Moses and our Joshua, going forth into battle for us, overthrowing kings on our behalf, and leading us into our own promised land.

"Jesus, lead Thou on, Till our rest is won" (*LSB* 718:1). Amen.

Like a Roaring Lion

Read 1 Peter 5:6–11

They open wide their mouths at Me, like a ravening and roaring lion. Psalm 22:13

When Peter wrote the words of today's reading, he might have had Psalm 22 in mind: "like a ravening and roaring lion." By comparing the devil to a roaring lion that wants to devour us, Peter allowed us to see that our dear Lord Jesus faced the same dangers we ourselves face. Jesus was surrounded by "roaring lions," as it were, ministers of Satan, who desired to overwhelm and destroy Him. When Jesus died, the lion thought he had won. However, the victory was only temporary. Christ has risen from the dead! He lives, and all His enemies shall be utterly defeated!

"Your adversary the devil prowls around like a roaring lion, seeking someone to devour." Where is the safest place for us to be? The safest place is near the cross of Christ, where the lion was silenced and rendered toothless.

Where can we go so that we may be as close as possible to the cross of Christ? We can go to the Lord's Supper where the benefits of the cross are served up for us: "For as often as you eat this bread and drink the cup, you proclaim the Lord's death [and victory over the devil] until He comes" (1 Corinthians 11:26).

I shall return, O Lord, by coming to Your table. Find me faithful. Amen.

Poured Out like Water

Read 1 John 5:6–11

> I am poured out like water, and all My bones are out of joint. Psalm 22:14

When John wrote the words of today's reading, he may have considered Psalm 22: "This is He who came by water and blood—Jesus Christ." John also reported in his Gospel, "One of the soldiers pierced His [Jesus'] side . . . and at once there came out blood and water" (John 19:34).

Martin Luther connected the blood and water to our forgiveness of sins. First, Luther stated, "The blood that flows out of Christ's side is the forgiveness of sins and our redemption" (AE 69:267). Then Luther continued:

> The water is the Holy Spirit who daily washes and purifies us through the Word. For even though we are baptized, believe in Christ, and have forgiveness of sins through faith in His blood, nevertheless we still have our flesh around our necks, flesh that is full of evil lusts and sins that fight against the Spirit. . . . That is why it is necessary that we be continually washed and purified. Through the blood we are redeemed. Through the water we are daily washed, cleansed, and purified. The blood accomplishes forgiveness of sins and redemption from all evil. The water accomplishes the cleansing of the remaining sins and evil lusts until we become entirely pure (AE 69:268).

"O Jesus, let Thy precious blood Be to my soul a cleansing flood" (LSB 613:3). Amen.

In the Dust of Death
Read Romans 3:21–26

My strength is dried up like a potsherd, and My tongue
sticks to My jaws; You lay Me in the dust of death.
Psalm 22:15

Artistic depictions of Christ on the cross sometimes also include images of God the Father and God the Holy Spirit in attendance. When God the Father is depicted at His Son's crucifixion, He is usually in human form: His hands are outstretched, either supporting the beam of the cross or pinning His Son in place while the Son expires. Thus, the Father is shown to be an active participant in the death of His Son, "whom God put forward as a propitiation by His blood" (Romans 3:25).

The Son knew about His Father's participation in His Son's death. Psalm 22 speaks prophetically about our Lord's plight on His cross. These words in particular speak about the Son's knowledge of His Father: "You lay Me in the dust of death." What extraordinary love! What extraordinary trust! In the same way that the Father placed all confidence in His Son, so the Son trusted His Father in all things— even when His Father laid Him "in the dust of death."

We can learn from Jesus. Rather than blaming God for everything that goes wrong, we can simply trust in Him—even when He lays us "in the dust of death."

Give me a goodly share of Your trust, O Lord. Amen.

Encircled

Read Matthew 26:47–56

For dogs encompass Me; a company of evildoers encircles Me; they have pierced My hands and feet. Psalm 22:16

In military strategy, a maneuver called *flanking* consists of attacking the sides or the rear of your enemy's position. If you are able to flank the enemy, you gain a great advantage because your enemy must now fight on multiple fronts. Defense becomes more difficult, and movement becomes nearly impossible. Flanking is one of the most successful military maneuvers in history: Hannibal of Carthage famously flanked the Roman Army at Cannae during the Second Punic War (216 BC), and military leaders have imitated the maneuver ever since. Even schoolyard bullies intuitively know that surrounding their victim will give them the advantage.

The enemies of our Lord had Him flanked: "a company of evildoers encircles Me." Even if our Lord had wished to launch a response (which He did not), there was no opportunity to mount a defense or make an escape. Jesus was outmaneuvered and closed in on all sides. His friends had all abandoned Him, and the legions of angels silently kept their swords sheathed. "All this has taken place that the Scriptures of the prophets might be fulfilled" (Matthew 26:56). In the crisis of the moment, our Lord's only option appeared also to be the worst of all options. It proved to be the best.

Help me, Lord, when I feel myself to be outflanked and encircled! Amen.

Lent
Week Five

I Can Count All My Bones

Read Exodus 12:43–51

I can count all My bones—they stare and gloat over
Me. Psalm 22:17

The phrase "I can count all My bones" is a figure of speech. They parallel the famous prophecy concerning Jesus on the cross, "He keeps all His bones; not one of them is broken" (Psalm 34:20; see also John 19:36). Recall the grisly work:

> Since it was the day of Preparation, and so that the bodies would not remain on the cross on the Sabbath (for that Sabbath was a high day), the Jews asked Pilate that their legs might be broken. . . . So the soldiers came and broke the legs of the first, and of the other who had been crucified with Him. But when they came to Jesus and saw that He was already dead, they did not break His legs. (John 19:31–33)

By means of His crucified Son's unbroken legs, God the Father was emphasizing the connection between Jesus and the Old Testament Passover lamb: "You shall not break any of its bones" (Exodus 12:46). Thus, the Scriptures teach—and we must believe—that the body of Jesus provides us with protection from God's condemning wrath. Jesus is our Passover Lamb. By eating His body, we are spared from death and delivered from the Egypt of our sins.

Thank You, heavenly Father, that You prepared for me the meal of my deliverance in the body of Your Son. Amen.

Roll the Dice

Read John 19:23–24

They divide My garments among them, and for My clothing they cast lots. Psalm 22:18

Our Lord's life was precious. "Deliver . . . My precious life!" (Psalm 22:20 But the soldiers at His cross had identified something that was more valuable than the life of our God: "The tunic was seamless, woven in one piece from top to bottom, so they said to one another, 'Let us not tear it'" (John 19:24). By casting their lots for His clothing, the soldiers demonstrated that they thought more highly of the materials they had received from Jesus than they thought of Jesus Himself. Him they nailed to a cross, seemingly without a second thought. His clothing was the object of their full attention and earnest desire.

The action of the soldiers might seem cold and crass. However, we should not be quick to condemn them, because we do the same thing. When we ask our heavenly Father for our daily bread, God opens His hand to satisfy our desires (Psalm 145:16). But then, like Roman soldiers at the foot of the cross, we easily turn our attention more acutely to the materials rather than to the One from whom all blessings flow.

God, forgive us! Grant us Your grace, despite our material desires! By Your Good Spirit, turn us away from the clothing and toward the Christ, in order that we may "receive our daily bread with thanksgiving" (Small Catechism, Fourth Petition, Lord's Prayer). Amen.

Come Quickly, Lord!
Read Revelation 22:12–21

But You, O LORD, do not be far off! O You My help, come
quickly to My aid! Psalm 22:19

The back porch on a warm, sunny day. Under a blanket on a win-
try night. On the beach in Acapulco. Where is your favorite place?
Why do you like to be there?

Alongside a busy highway, changing a tire in the darkness of a
rainy night. In a hospital room or a prison cell. Enclosed in a casket.
Where do you most dread to be? Why don't you want to be there?

When we are surrounded by comforts, it is easy to remain. When
we are fearful, sorrowful, and filled with pain, it is easy to want something different. Perhaps that is why the Lord our God allows us our
discomforts, our terrors, and our pains. He wants us to long for something more than what we now have. He wants us to focus on the coming of our Lord on the Last Day. Maranatha! Come quickly, Lord!

Our Lord Jesus was stripped of all comforts and of every reason
to enjoy His position. Jesus was required to wait upon the Lord just
as we must wait. Jesus called upon the Lord, as we must, and the Lord
heard Him. This gives us the hope that we, too, shall be heard.

Help me, Lord, always to return. Even more so, Lord, return to me! Amen.

My Precious Life

Read Revelation 12:7–12

Deliver My soul from the sword, My precious life from
the power of the dog! Psalm 22:20

Our Lord Jesus loved His life. His life was so dear to Him—so
cherished by Him—that the psalmist could say, "Deliver . . . My precious life!" Yet, as personally valuable as our Lord's life was to Him, He
"loved not His life even unto death," to paraphrase Revelation 12:11.

Most people do not wish to die. Even when their bodies have been
devastated by illness or injury; even after all their friends and family have abandoned them or gone forward into death before them;
even in times of "distress, or persecution, or famine, or nakedness, or
danger, or sword" (Romans 8:35), the will to live can remain strong.
Why? Because life is precious. Your life is precious to you. My life is
precious to me. Our Lord's life was precious to Him.

What did Jesus give when He died on the cross? Jesus gave the
most precious gift He was able to give. Why did Jesus give this gift?
Because there were things that He considered more precious than His
body and life. He "loved not His life even unto death" because He
loved us all the more.

I love You, Jesus, but not nearly as much as You love me. Help me "love
not my life unto death" that I may die trusting You and confessing Your
name. Amen.

You Have Rescued Me

Read Isaiah 53:1–12

Save Me from the mouth of the lion! You have rescued
Me from the horns of the wild oxen! Psalm 22:21

The prophet Isaiah lived hundreds of years before the birth of Jesus. However, when Isaiah famously prophesied the death and resurrection of our Lord, he wrote in the past tense: "He [Jesus] *was* despised and rejected by men. . . . He *was* wounded for our transgression; He *was* crushed for our iniquities." (Isaiah 53:3, 5, emphasis added).

Why did Isaiah write in the past tense about things that would take place in the future, hundreds of years after their writing? Theologians and Bible scholars call it the "prophetic past." Isaiah wrote in the past tense to express the absolute certainty of the prophecy, to emphasize the unwavering reliability of God's words and promises. In Isaiah's mouth, Jesus "was wounded for our transgressions" because the deed was as good as done, even though (historically speaking) it was still yet to be done.

Psalm 22 speaks the same "prophetic past." Psalm 22 speaks the voice of Jesus on His cross. Even before He died, our Lord knew His resurrection was an absolute certainty! His resurrection was so certain that it could be described in the past tense: "You have rescued Me from the horns of the wild oxen!"

Give me Your Holy Spirit, heavenly Father, that I may trust Your promises as absolutely as Your Son trusted them. Amen.

I Will

Read John 20:11–17

I will tell of Your name to My brothers; in the midst of
the congregation I will praise You. Psalm 22:22

The words "I will tell of Your name" and "I will praise you" speak about the hope and certainty of Christ's resurrection from the dead. Psalm 22 speaks in our Lord's voice, describing His agony and death on the cross. For any observer at Golgotha, all hope was gone for that crucified man who had proclaimed Himself to be King of the Jews. As far as the observer would have been concerned, there was no future for that man, no possibility of escape, and no reasonable way that He could speak confidently about anything except death.

Yet Jesus lived in hope, even in the waning moments of His life! "I will tell of Your name to My brothers; in the midst of the congregation I will praise You." These words mirror Job's confession of the resurrection: "After my skin has been thus destroyed, yet in my flesh I shall see God, whom I shall see for myself, and my eyes shall behold, and not another. My heart faints within me!" (Job 19:25–26).

Dearest Jesus, You returned from death by the power of the resurrection, telling God's name to Your brothers and praising Him in the midst of the congregation. Return me also from the dust and ashes that I may do the same in the great assembly of eternal life. Amen.

Awe

Read Psalm 99

You who fear the LORD, praise Him! All you offspring of Jacob, glorify Him, and stand in awe of Him, all you offspring of Israel! Psalm 22:23

Perhaps there are some words that should be reserved for use exclusively for the praise of the Lord our God. The words *awe* and *awesome* might be a couple of examples. In our everyday speech, *awesome* can equally describe a beautiful sunrise, our child's good grades, or the latest trick from the skateboarder who lives up the street. In our advertising-driven world, where everything gets expressed in the most superlative forms possible, *awe* and *awesome* lose their significance.

Our God is "a great and awesome God" (Deuteronomy 7:21) who has a "great and awesome name" (Psalm 99:3), does "great and awesome things" (1 Chronicles 17:21), and "is clothed with awesome majesty" (Job 37:22). There is nothing more awesome than the death of our Lord for the sin of the world. "Stand in awe of Him, all you offspring of Israel!"

Skateboard tricks are amazing to watch. A glorious sunrise fills our eyes with wonder and joy. Good grades create feelings of pride and happiness. Our God alone, crucified and resurrected for us and for our salvation, is truly awesome.

Help me to reflect upon the true awesomeness of Your Word and works, O Lord, that all other things may fall into a better perspective for me. Amen.

Lent
Holy Week

He Has Heard

Read James 5:7–12

For He has not despised or abhorred the affliction of
the afflicted, and He has not hidden His face from Him,
but has heard, when He cried to Him. Psalm 22:24

God the Father in heaven did not seem to be paying attention. His only-begotten Son, the One in whom He was well pleased, hung expiring on the cross. Yet Psalm 22 indicates that the heavenly Father, indeed, fully heard His Son's perfect prayers: "He has not hidden His face from Him, but has heard, when He cried to Him."

Here we can learn about our heavenly Father's responses to the prayers we also pray. Just because our Father does not jump to His feet and rush to make everything the way we personally want it to be does not mean that He has failed to hear our prayers. Jesus prayed, and then Jesus waited. God's answer to His Son's prayer was not no, but wait.

Jesus promised us, "Whatever you ask in prayer, you will receive, if you have faith" (Matthew 21:22). Why, then, have we not yet received? Not because Jesus spoke falsely but because we have not yet waited. God has heard your prayer, just as He heard our Lord's prayers. God answered His Son. He shall answer you.

Help me, O Lord, to return to my prayers, which You have promised to hear. Answer me, O Lord, in Your own time and according to Your good pleasure. Amen.

My Vows I Will Perform
Read James 4:13–17

From You comes My praise in the great congregation;
My vows I will perform before those who fear Him.
Psalm 22:25

Because of the persistence of our selfish nature, we tend to confuse God's will with our personal will. We seize upon an idea or desire that we find attractive. Because we find it attractive, we naturally assume that it came from God, spoken and inspired by the Holy Spirit. That is why James instructed, "You ought to say, 'If the Lord wills, we will live and do this or that'" (James 4:15). Rather than immediately thinking every notion that enters our head is God's will, we must hold our peace, wait upon the Lord, and see how things work out.

Psalm 22 declared in the voice of our crucified Lord, "My vows I will perform." There was no "If the Lord wills . . ." added to the declaration. It was the will of the Lord that Jesus be crucified. It was also the will of the Lord that Jesus be raised again on Easter Sunday. Jesus perfectly knew the will of the Lord. Therefore, while He painfully died, He also declared in confidence, "My vows I will perform before those who fear Him." Then Jesus waited upon the Lord, as we must wait. Thus, Jesus sanctified our waiting.

Return me to the Scriptures, dear Lord Jesus, and help me to wait. Amen.

The Food of the Afflicted

Read Isaiah 25:6–12

The afflicted shall eat and be satisfied; those who seek
Him shall praise the LORD! May your hearts live forever!
Psalm 22:26

The Old Testament contains several odd-sounding references to eating. For example, when Moses, Aaron, and the elders of Israel approached the presence of God on Mount Sinai, they did not merely see God: "They beheld God, and ate and drank" (Exodus 24:11). David and his men ate the holy bread of the Presence without fear of condemnation (1 Samuel 21:6). Psalm 22, spoken in the voice of the crucified Christ, likewise promised, "The afflicted shall eat and be satisfied."

These references to eating might be Old Testament shadows or echoes of the Lord's Supper, which Jesus gave to us on the night He was betrayed. "This is My body . . . this is My blood" (Matthew 26:26, 28). In the Lord's Supper, we eat in the presence of God, as did Moses and the elders; there we take the holy bread along with David and his men; there we find true satisfaction for our afflictions. In the Lord's Supper, we see the distant fulfillment of Isaiah's prophecy yet to be fulfilled on the Last Day. "On this mountain the Lord of hosts will make for all peoples a feast of rich food, a feast of well-aged wine, of rich food full of marrow, of aged wine well refined" (Isaiah 25:6).

Feed me, Jesus, that I may hunger no more. Amen.

Turn to the Lord

Read Matthew 4:12–17

All the ends of the earth shall remember and turn to the LORD, and all the families of the nations shall worship before You. Psalm 22:27

John the Baptist preached, "Repent, for the kingdom of heaven is at hand" (Matthew 3:2). Christ Jesus our Lord took up the same sermon, likewise declaring, "Repent for the kingdom of heaven is at hand" (Matthew 4:17). When the disciples of our Lord went out, they "proclaimed that people should repent" (Mark 6:12). After the resurrection of Jesus, the disciples-turned-apostles were sent again "that repentance for the forgiveness of sins should be proclaimed in His [Jesus'] name to all nations, beginning from Jerusalem" (Luke 24:47).

All preaching eventually boils down to repentance, which means "turning." Thus, all preaching originates from the cross. After all, Psalm 22 speaks in the voice of Jesus from the cross: "All the ends of the earth shall remember and turn to the LORD." This could be why Paul so emphatically declared, "We preach Christ crucified!" (1 Corinthians 1:23)

"The word of the cross . . . is the power of God" (1 Corinthians 1:18). The Word of the cross is the power of our turning. The Word concerning the crucified Christ is the power of the Holy Spirit, who turns us away from our sin and back toward the One who died for our sins.

Come, Holy Spirit! Turn me and my family that we may remember the Lord. Amen.

He Rules Over the Nations

Read Romans 13:1–7

For kingship belongs to the LORD, and He rules over the nations. Psalm 22:28

Jesus said to Pontius Pilate, "You would have no authority over Me at all unless it had been given you from above" (John 19:11). Prior to that, Jesus prayed, "Father . . . glorify Your Son that the Son may glorify You, since You have given Him authority over all flesh" (John 17:1–2). These words of Jesus indicate that all governing power in this world comes from the Father through the Son. That is why Paul also wrote, "There is no authority except from God, and those that exist have been instituted by God" (Romans 13:1).

"For kingship belongs to the LORD, and He rules over the nations." These words give twofold comfort. First, the death of Jesus was not something that had gone awry or had taken place by means of usurped authority. No. "Kingship belongs to the LORD," and the Lord knew exactly what was taking place when Jesus died. The death of Christ was planned and sanctioned from above.

The second comfort has to do with our lives in the political realm today. One thing remains eternally true—no matter what happens, who takes office, what tax burden gets imposed, or which government falls—"He rules over the nations." We are neither alone nor forgotten.

Nations rise and fall, O Lord! Continually return me to the truth that You alone are Lord of the nations. Amen.

The Prosperous
Read 1 Corinthians 3:18–23

All the prosperous of the earth eat and worship; before
Him shall bow all who go down to the dust, even the
one who could not keep himself alive. Psalm 22:29

The words "the prosperous of the earth" refer to you, me, and the entire Christian Church. We know that we are "the prosperous" because we are the ones who "eat and worship" on account of the sacrificial death of our Lord. We worship God without fear because "the blood of Jesus His Son cleanses us from all sin" (1 John 1:7, see also Luke 1:74). We miraculously participate in His crucified body when we eat the Lord's Supper (1 Corinthians 10:16). Thus, the Scriptures are fulfilled: "All the prosperous of the earth eat and worship."

All God's people are His prosperous ones too. Our prosperity has nothing to do with the amount of daily bread God has given to this or that Christian. To be sure, in an earthly and superficial sense, some Christians are richer in materials while others are poorer. (God did this for the purpose of neighborly love.) However, we have each been made completely prosperous in Him. Our prosperity in Christ is a declared prosperity, just as our forgiveness of sins is declared to us. All things belong to our Christ, and our Christ now belongs to us. We truly lack nothing while we await our inheritance in heaven.

Lord, thank You for my prosperity. Amen.

The Coming Generation
Read Luke 16:1–13

Posterity shall serve Him; it shall be told of the Lord to
the coming generation. Psalm 22:30

In our everyday usage, the word *generation* refers to a group of people who were all born at roughly the same time. Thus, we speak of the Baby Boomers (1946–1964), Generation X (1965–1979), and the Xennials (1975–1985).

Jesus sometimes used the word *generation* in a different way, not to classify people according to age but according to faith or unbelief. For example, "An evil and adulterous generation seeks for a sign" (Matthew 12:39). Again, "The sons of this world are more shrewd in dealing with their own generation than the sons of light" (Luke 16:8). These uses of *generation* refer to that group of people who are joined together by unbelief, not by age.

Understanding *generation* as a reference to faith or unbelief can help our reading of Psalm 22. "It shall be told of the Lord to the coming generation" does not need to refer only to those first Christians who heard the news of our Lord's death and resurrection. "The coming generation" can include all those who hear the Word of the cross and believe, no matter what year they were born. We Christians are the posterity that "shall serve Him" because the Good News of God in Christ has been delivered to us, and we have heard it.

Thank You, Jesus, for adding me to the generation of those who believe.
Amen.

He Has Done It!

Read Luke 24:36–53

They shall come and proclaim His righteousness to a
people yet unborn, that He has done it. Psalm 22:31

The word *they* includes the disciples of our Lord who were sent
out as His apostles "in Jerusalem and in all Judea and Samaria, and to
the end of the earth" (Acts 1:8). The preaching done by the apostles
has become our New Testament by which we hear the joyous news
"Christ is risen! He is risen, indeed! Alleluia!" The original eyewit-
nesses of Jesus, through their Spirit-empowered words, still today
"proclaim His righteousness to a people yet unborn, that He has done
it."

What exactly has God done? God has vindicated and saved the
entire world through the suffering and death of His Son, which was
described in painful detail in every line of Psalm 22! But now the pain
is over; now the agony has ended; now death and hell have met their
match!

Two thousand years later, the message of forgiveness and life still
shines forth. Everything needed for our forgiveness of sins, salvation,
and eternal life was fully completed for us long before we were born.

Mighty Victim from the sky, Hell's fierce pow'rs beneath You lie; You have
conquered in the fight, You have brought us life and light! Alleluia! Now
no more can death appall, Now no more the grave enthrall; You have
opened paradise, And Your saints in You shall rise. Alleluia! (*LSB* 633:5–6).